HISTORIOLA

ISBN 978-1-914166-04-4 (Hardcover)
ISBN 978-1-914166-05-1 (Paperback)

A catalogue for this title is available from the British Library.

10 9 8 7 6 5 4 3 2 1

Hardcover edition printed by Biddles, Norfolk.
First published in 2021
Hadean Press
West Yorkshire
England

www.hadeanpress.com

HISTORIOLA

The Power of Narrative Charms

Carl Nordblom

This book is dedicated to Johannes Björn Gårdbäck, for his excellent transmission of the magical arts. All good ideas found in this work should be credited to him, and all the bad ones should be ascribed to me.

CONTENTS

INTRODUCTION

Så sant som sagt
(As true as said)
Traditional Swedish folk charm

For each and every one of us, words and images are fundamental to how reality is experienced. As universal means of expression and meaning, they are not only symbolic, but also carriers of information and power. They can change our minds, and they can change the world. They alter our perception as much as they are the very way through which we experience ourselves and everything around us. As we navigate through our inner and outer worlds we also clothe them in words and images, be this for good or for bad. These are the stories, myths, and charms which speak forth the moment, perpetually appearing in new, wonderful and terrible forms. From the mirror-image to the idol, the subject to the object, the enchantments woven by the threads of words and images both fetter as well as shelter us. Yet by their ever-changing forms and fluidity, we always have the chance to weave new garlands to dress our world. The artists and poets know this, as they are ever enraptured in the sowing of new, bewildering masks and costumes. So do the sophists and politicians, concealing the naked monarch under their illusionary guises. The philosophers stare themselves blind at the patchwork, trying to discover the meaning gone into the stiches, whilst the mystics tear at them as coverings of a truth hidden beneath the veils.

The magicians on the other hand understand words and images – as they do the world in general – as expressions and carriers of *power*. For them the word is a possibility of fixing dynamic energy, like the linguist fixes meaning. Likewise, the image is another formulation of power, a vessel to embody the direct force of spirit or consciousness. The practice of magic can thus be seen as a matter of tracing and depicting words and images for things which are not usually grasped by the ordinary man. This is done for a number of purposes, be it to communicate with these generally hidden aspects of reality, to control or manipulate them, or simply to have a reference for them so they can be avoided. When experiencing that which is foreign, we give it a word and/or an image so that it can be manageable for us to interact with, and so that it can be spoken about and spoken to, otherwise it must continue to remain foreign and strange to us. This is because magic does not just describe the world, giving it superficial meanings and definitions but, more importantly, seeks to make the foreign accessible to us so that the occulted may become visible and graspable.

On the surface this might sound somewhat similar to the theories found within sociology and post-structural thought: namely that words and images are used to display and communicate social power-structures.[1] They shape and are shaped by underlying discursive tendencies which uphold world-views and are thus highly linked to how certain social groups both empower themselves as well as dominate others. Yet within magical practice we are mainly talking about power in a more 'hands on' sense, similar to how a smith or a carpenter knows how to apply force to a material through the use of their tools. The main difference is that the practice of magic is working with a lot more subtle materials and makes use

---

1 See the works of Roland Barthes, Jacques Derrida, Michel Foucault, et al.

of a lot more subtle tools. Power is made readily available to the magician by means of certain methods and techniques, as they navigate the unseen forces of the universe for whatever end they see fit. Thus, the magical view of the world is a perspective of the movement and establishment of force, where every single thing has a potential to be practically ready-at-hand. For example, a healer is someone who can locate and find the subtle root of an underlying issue for a client, and then treat this issue. In magical practice, both the diagnosis as well as the treatment can be done by the use of words of power as well as images. The words may be spoken charms, conjurations, or incantations, while the images may be those which appear before the 'mind's eye', actual visual signs or the physical images made to 'represent' the client, the illness, or the treatment. The list of how one may apply words and images to the practice is almost infinite in number, as this is a matter of personal technique, cultural context, and tradition.

When creating visual and verbal structures, the signs and stories help us organize a specific situation so that we can approach it practically. There must thus be something of a terminology in use, a framework for the practice, in order for us to work with it in a meaningful and controlled manner, otherwise we have to redefine our stance continuously as we go along. This structure is informed by our wider world-view and specific cultural context, which have already established a rich set of words and symbols. Perhaps most importantly here is the religious world of the person in relation to the more general socio-political and purely material dimensions that must be taken into account for how they come to describe their experiences and establish their practices. As magic seeks to interact with subtle forces, the definitions presented in their own general established cultic milieu of, for instance, subtle entities and their place in the cosmos, are highly useful. Moving into the direct terrain of magical practice, we meet a more specific plethora of established terms and teachings that are meant to support the practitioners in their work. These are produced and embodied via tradition, as they are tried and tested in a living reality by those using them. The magical images and words are, in that sense, both reliant on the web of meanings which we find ourselves in as partakers of various 'worlds' and traditions, but also highly connected to a subjective level of experience via their actual application by practitioners in a lived real-world setting.

To understand the function and application of the magical images and words, we must be able to link these two spheres together, looking at both the broader cultural significance of their function, as well as the subjective experience of the working practitioner who uses them in action. If not, we will neither come to terms with why certain signs and words are being used in a magical context, nor how they are conceived to have worked by the magician. By exploring the methodology of magic in this way, it will be shown how profound it can be and how it utterly redefines the presumed ideas of the theoretician of language and culture.

This book focuses on a very particular form of a spoken or written charm which is formulated as a narrative. Within modern academia this is termed a *historiola*, and it has been discussed at some length by scholars in order to classify various forms of textual sources within the study of ancient and modern magic.[2] Other scholars have, however, come to explore the actual methodology of the narrated charms in terms of 'explaining' the underlying linguistic and philosophical ideas at work in this practice. Here we usually see theories taken from recent studies in 'post-Wittgensteinian' philosophy of language. Although some of the arguments and ideas presented among such papers are interesting and perhaps valuable within a purely academic *milieu*, as a practitioner of

---

2 See Frankfurter, Graf, Bozóky, Kropp, et al.

narrative charms, I find them more than begging in their rather 'arm-chair' understanding of how magic actually works. This book is thus an attempt to move the discourse from the purely academic, which has been mainly preoccupied with approaching historical textual sources, into a more nuanced understanding of the narrative charms as a living practice. My approach begins with my personal experiences of these practices found within my native tradition, while exploring the history and variations of the *historiolae* within other cultural settings. The approach could thus be seen as phenomenological in essence, as well as comparative in that I explore a wide range of textual sources found among the works of contemporary scholars of religion. It should be noted that with this I am not seeking to justify or defend my practice via the theoretical terms which academia has already established, but am rather sharing my own thoughts on what I view as a beautiful and extremely potent form of sorcery. Hopefully this work might also be of some help to fellow practitioners in some way or another, either in the sense that they might come to explore *historiolae* in their own traditions, or perhaps simply to give them some food for thought.

It should also be noted that the ideas expressed here are informed by the way in which I have been taught these practices and how they were presented to me by my teacher, as well as by how I have come to understand them through my own practice. Traditionally, these types of charms have been handed down to us by specialists as well as 'common folk', perhaps neither of whom were interested in digging too deeply into the theoretical side of their craft. Although most people will at least ponder the nature of how their own methods work, these charms are (as previously noted) examples of a 'hands-on' approach to magic where little time is given to contemplation about lofty metaphysical matters and the focus has rather been on curing dire illness, driving off what was perceived as life-threatening harm. As such, it is of utter importance that we treat these methods with the care and respect they deserve, as they are not only testimonials of the great power and wit of our ancestors, but also highly useful forms of healing and hexing for the contemporary magician.

Narrative Troll Formulas

I first came across charms written in the form of narratives when studying my native folk magical tradition commonly called *Trolldom*. This is a tradition which emerges out of the Norse countries of Sweden, Finland, Norway, and Denmark, and contains a large number of magical methods to heal and protect people and livestock, divine the future, or communicate with spirits of nature and the dead. Both the means and the aims of these practices are directly connected with the farm and the rural household, as well as the popular beliefs of post-Catholic Scandinavia. Most of the collected written sources which we find in the so-called *Svartkonstböcker* (black arts books) or *Cyprianus Books* (named after St. Cyprian of Antioch) have thus come to solidify a specific type of magical tradition in the way in which it was practiced over roughly the last five-hundred years or so. As will be explored later on, however, there are plenty of methods and material among these written sources which stem from much earlier practices used among the Scandinavians.

Among the documented incantations and charms referred to as troll formulas (sv. *trollformler*) there are plenty of examples of what can be described as magical narratives, usually following similar structures or frame stories which can be slightly varied in form and function depending on the aim of the charm and its specific context. These types of charms have in modern academic scholarship been named *historiolae*, which have been defined as:

('Little story'). Modern term describing brief tales built into magic formulas, providing a mythic precedence for a magically effective treatment.[3]

Similarly, within the Trolldom tradition, these commonly appear as very short tales where protagonists such as Jesus, a saint, or some other powerful mythological character takes on the task of healing an injury or driving off a malign entity. Below are two examples of this type of troll formula documented in Scandinavia during the early modern period:

Against the evil eye

Jesus walked over the bridge the bridge so wide,
There he met the evil envy.
Where are you going? asked Jesus.
I shall go to that man's house
And hinder all he has.
No, said Jesus,
I shall turn thee myself
To the one who sent thee out.
You shall, until the end of the world,
In the blue mountain,
There you shall stand
Until Doomsday morning.
In three names (Father, Son, and Holy Spirit)[4]

---

3 Fritz Graf (Columbus, OH), 'Historiola', in: Brill's New Pauly, Antiquity volumes, ed. by Hubert Cancik and Helmuth Schneider, English Edition by Christine F. Salazar, Classical Tradition volumes ed. by Manfred Landfester, English Edition by Francis G. Gentry. First published online: 2006, <http://dx.doi.org/10.1163/1574-9347_bnp_e515850>.

4 Johannes Björn Gårdbäck, *Trolldom: Spells and Methods of the Norse Folk Magic Tradition* (YIPPIE, 2015), p. 119.

Against snake-bite

Our Lord Jesus walked along the road,
There lay a snake on the path
Lord Jesus said to the snake:
'Why do you sting people?
I will bind your jaw
I will deafen your sting
I will deafen your poison,
So much that there will be smoke
Like dew before the sun'[5]

They also appear in an even more direct manner, which the Swedish folk magician Johannes Gårdbäck described as 'the walk narrative formulas' where '… there is no meeting, only action'.[6]

Against strain

There came maidens wandering,
The first was the Sun,
The second the Moon,
The third was Virgin Mary.
They bound the bad uterus
With silver thread
With gold thread
As firm as the spirit
[Is bound] in the chains of the Dark Valley[7]

---

5 Norway 1800. Anton Christian Bang, *Norske Hexeformularer og Magiske Opskrifter* (Norway: Kristiania 1902), p. 160.

6 Gårdbäck, *Trolldom*, p. 75.

7 Bang, *Norske Hexeformularer og Magiske Opskrifter*, pp. 140-141.

Jesus and St. Peter rode over the mountains
Then his horse fell
And twisted its foot
Thus he bound
Flesh to Flesh
And Bone to Bone
In the name of God the Father, God's Son
and God the Holy Spirit. Amen.[8]

As I first read these intriguing little 'stories' I felt that they had a certain allure to them; they appeared to me to be steeped in a mixture of both 'rustic' and 'mystical' wording which I associated with the Trolldom tradition of Scandinavia. I was not, however, certain how these stories were supposed to be used, nor why they had the tendency to be written as mythical narratives. They seemed to contain many enigmatic and bewildering features, references and expressions that were hard to make sense of. First of all, I had never heard of any commonly known myths where, for instance, Jesus healed horses, or where the Virgin Mary, with the help of the sun and the moon, cured a bad uterus by binding it with thread. I could, however, identify some of the references, such as the 'blue mountain' mentioned in the first charm quoted above. Within Swedish folklore, this is the place located at the 'end of the world', where all witches, devils, and wicked beings in general are said to congregate during Maundy Thursday. On the other hand, the expression 'as dew before the sun', mentioned in the charm against snake-bite, made sense purely as an analogy: like early-morning dew evaporates and disappears as the sun rises, so does the narrator wish the poison of the snake to be gone from the victim. Yet why not simply refrain from using a narrative and just state this analogy explicitly?

---

8 Norway, 1668. Bang, *Norske Hexeformularer og Magiske Opskrifter*, p. 2.

Unlike more ceremonial forms of magic, here no spirits or powerful beings are summoned and compelled or commanded to perform an action on behalf of the magician. Within these charms such beings are fully established characters locked within a highly specified pattern of performances and events, seemingly located beyond the world of the person uttering them. In that sense, they almost appear closer to folk tales and short myths than to conjurations and spells as they are popularly conceived today. From a reductionist perspective, myths can be understood as cautionary or entertaining tales. They combine pure entertainment, primitive cosmology, and distant memories of history, and are also used to explain 'why things are as they are'. On the other hand, another perspective, more popular among esoteric and spiritually-minded authors is that myths should be seen as symbolic representations of the inner working of a spiritual reality. They reveal information about the nature of gods and heroes so that we can better understand them. However, both of these views seem to define a myth as a story that sets out to teach us something, helping us to make sense of the world and our place in it. The utility of the myth lies beyond its surface content, and it needs to be unraveled either by reduction or by a more esoteric reading of it.

Yet the mythical formulas which I found in the Trolldom tradition could not be understood to function like this at all. They did not seem to carry any notable teaching, other than being descriptive of a certain type of magical action. This, to some extent, follows the definition of the *historiola* previously quoted, as they function in 'providing a mythic precedence for a magically effective treatment'. Sometimes these appear explicitly, as in the charms retelling how a saint would ward off a specific demonic entity, which could perhaps be seen as examples of analogous events to be copied by the magician. As such, their recitation would function as so-called 'sympathetic magic'. This term, coined by the famous anthropologist Sir James Frazer, formulates a process of magic where one thing 'stands' for something else. In this line of thought an effigy in the form of a puppet, for instance, is crafted and used in a magical operation as a type of sympathetic link to the actual victim. The puppet acts by depicting and resembling the real life person; Frazer understood this to mean that in the 'primitive' mind of the magician the mere imitating action of sticking pins into a doll would likewise have a similar effect on the victim in question. The crucial idea here is that 'like produces like, or that an effect resembles its cause'.[9] We could perhaps apply this to the narrative charms, as their content obviously *resembles* the healing event wished by the healer. The myth could then be thought to not only explain the procedure of healing, but to function as an analogy of how a powerful entity performed it in a mythological time, and thus to aid the magician as a type of sympathetic link. There are several notable examples of a direct verbalization of such analogies in the formulas themselves:

For toothache

As surely as Moses stopped the water in the Red Sea, just
as surely I stop you[r] toothache for you, NN.
In the name of God the Father and of the Son and of
the Holy Ghost.[10]

For ache, toothache and other pain

The Virgin Mary stood at the Cross of Jesus and as
surely as she stood there, so surely shall this pain go

---

9 Sir James George Frazer, *The Golden Bough: The Magic Art* Vol. 1 (New York: MacMillan & Co., 1951), p. 52.

10 Dr. Thomas K. Johnson, *Svartkonstböcker : A Compendium of the Swedish Black Art Book Tradition* (Seattle: Revelore Press, 2019) p. 313.

away, that say I N.N. In the name of God the Father and
of the Son and of the Holy Ghost.[11]

To still blood
Stand blood to blood as Jordan's flood
Shall still stand as for Jesus stood[12]

Note how these charms first describe a mythical event and
then directly state that they should function in the same way as the
action undertaken by the magician. There are plenty of variations
to be found though, and sometimes it can be somewhat difficult to
see where a charm is purely in the form of a mythical narrative and
where the overlap is between the actions of the magician and the
actions of the saintly figure:

To bind a snake
Virgin Mary gave me a chord
And asked me to bind the snake
'I bind the head
I bind the skull
I bind all that,
That may hurt me
You shall lie,
Lie so still,
From head to tail'[13]

---

11 Johnson, *Svartkonstböcker*, p. 345.

12 Ferdinand Ohrt, *Danmarks Trylleformler* Vol 1-2 (Gyldendal, 1917), p. 150.

13 Bang, *Norske Hexeformularer og Magiske Opskrifter*, p. 164.

As well as offering a narrative and a sort of 'sympathetic link' or analogy to the magician, we also find what we could call a *formula proper* uttered by the Virgin Mary within this particular narrative. One could deduce that the narrative is nothing more than a mere frame-story and that the main source of magical power lies in nothing else than the narrated words at the end. Most of the previous examples at least include the use of the names of the divine trinity, which similarly could be thought to be the actual effective means which brings about the healing. However, not all of the charms include a narrative reference to the magician, nor do all of them include a formula spoken by the narrated protagonist. As for the use of the three names of the trinity, these rather seem to be used as either mere *formalia* or more probably as a type of amplification as *voces magicae* or words of power; if they were the only source of power it would seem strange that they had to be used alongside a further series of words. Perhaps most striking are the so-called 'walk narrative formulas' which only have a narrative, and sometimes even lack either direct words of power or a spoken formula by the protagonist.

ୡ

It seems to me that there is a high sense of inventiveness and creativity that has gone into the construction of these charms, and that various forms of 'building blocks' of magical wording are at use in them. Some of these include the very *voces magicae*, and some of them include the magical formula *proper,* or both of these, or even none of these, yet they all make use of a narrative in one sense or another. It appears, then, that these narratives have a conceived magical function *in and of themselves.* So although the charm can be constructed using several different components, when established within a narrative context, the whole of the charm must be thought to function as *voces magicae*, a formula proper and a narrative all in one. The narrative not only binds the other parts together, but as it can function on its own, it brings yet another ingredient to the charm. Most clearly this ingredient can be understood as the establishment of formalized action and movement.

During the course of my own studies and practice of these charms, this notion has become directly affirmed, mainly due to the techniques that were entrusted to me by my teacher. It is the very narrative itself that helps create the dynamism of the spell, enabling a direct 'movement' of the ritual procedure which is sometimes difficult to access otherwise. The narrative grants the magician access to a process as well as an end goal: it defines a procedure of magical action and at the same time executes it. Without having to summon high powers and ask/beg/bargain/ threaten them to do your bidding, one is instead immediately granted access to their power, which can be applied to a vast number of given situations. By observing the inner dynamics and processes of the charms in action, I quickly came to view them as some of the most potent forms of folk magic I had encountered, and their metaphysical implications to be so astounding that they could easily be used as a brilliant example to establish something of a general phenomenology of magic. Instead of perceiving them as functioning as 'sympathetic magic' or mere analogies, I came to view them rather as something like magical machineries of great power, which combined the processes of verbal and visual magic with the ritual application of story-telling and myth.

To fully demonstrate this notion, however, it is useful to get a better grip on how these charms are related to cultural and religious contexts, and how they make use of mythical figures and scenarios. As we shall see, this will tell us something about how these narrative charms have been constructed and what materials practitioners have drawn from in order to establish meaning and functionality. In the following chapter I will examine the historical roots of the troll formulas in order to answer why these charms make use of narrative and myth as they do.

HISTORICAL HISTORIOLAE

In 1841 two incantations written in High German in the 10th century were found in Merseburg. The first of them is to be used in order to escape bonds, and reads as follows:

> The Idisi [women/maiden] once alighted,
> alighted yonder.
> Some riveted fetters, others stemmed the war tide,
> Others hammered upon the chains:
> Slip from the shackles, escape from the foe![14]

Like some of the later Scandinavian charms, this one narrates an action performed by a group of women. No words of power are spoken, and the efficacy of the charm seems simply to lie in the narrative itself. When looking at the characters in the narrative, we can perhaps see a similarity with the example of the early modern Norse charm which began with the words *'There came maidens wandering...'* quoted earlier. There are plenty of similar troll formulas recorded, and the story of three women appearing seemingly out of nowhere and coming to the rescue seems to have been a very popular one, found not only in Scandinavia but also across all of Europe. In several examples of this type of mythic incantation, the first two of the maidens perform actions opposite to, or without benefitting the purpose of the help needed, while the third maiden always gets it right. Here is an example recorded in 1891 on the Isle of Man:

---

14 Felix Grendon, 'The Anglo-Saxon Charms', *Journal of American Folklore* 22.84 (University of Toronto, 1909), 110.

Three godly men came from Rome – Christ, Peter, and
Paul. Christ was on the cross, his blood flowing, and
Mary on her knees close by. One took the enchanted one
in his right hand, and Christ drew a cross ✠ over him.
Three young women came over the water, one of them
said 'up,' another one said, 'stay,' and the third one said
'I will stop the blood of man or woman.' Me to say it,
and Christ to do it, in the name of the Father, and the
Son, and the Holy Ghost.[15]

The third of the three maidens whom we meet here is usually
identified as the Virgin Mary in the later charms, yet sometimes
(as we have seen) the three remain nameless. Perhaps they can be
thought to be 'the three Marys', as in the Virgin Mother, Mary
Cleophas (sometimes identified as the Virgin Mary's sister-in-law)
and Mary Magdalene.[16] Yet these three ladies in their unnamed
form can be found in even earlier charms written in Latin, and
it is notable that they are highly connected to the art of weaving,
binding and releasing knots. The first of the following two charms
was recorded by Marcellus Empiricus in the 5th century, and the
second in *Medicina Plinii* in the 4th century:

There was a tree in the middle of the sea and hanging
from it was a bucket of human intestines; three virgins
went around it, two knotted them, one unraveled them.[17]

15 A.W. Moore quoted by Owen Davies in 'Healing Charms in Use in
England and Wales 1700-1950', *Folklore*, 107:1-2, 21.

16 Owen Davies, 'Healing Charms in Use in England and Wales 1700-
1950', *Folklore*, 107:1-2, 29.

17 Edina Bozóky, 'Medieval Narrative Charms', in *The Power of Words:
Studies on Charms and Charming in Europe*, ed. by J. Kapaló, É. Pócs & W.
Ryan (Budapest: Central European University Press, 2013) p. 111.

Three sisters were walking; one was turning, the second separating, the third dissolving.[18]

It is curious to note that the three women we meet in these charms are more similar to the *Moira* or *Norns,* found in Greek and Germanic myth respectively, than anything else. These maidens

---

18 Bozóky, 'Medieval Narrative Charms', p. 111.

are usually understood as mighty goddesses of fate, who weave the threads of destiny. In the charm narratives they use their abilities to spin, bind, and dissolve for all kinds of purposes, be it to sew together wounds, to break fetters, or to heal a bad uterus. Yet we should not find it strange that their presence continues in later medieval and early modern times under a different guise, as even though the pre-Christian beliefs came to fade, their function as great healers and breakers of bonds remained. The three Marys thus came to overtake their practice to fit within the current religious and cultural context, as there was still a need for these three Christian saints to provide a service similar to that which their pagan predecessors had offered.

An even more obvious example of such a process of change and assimilation into a Christian context can be found in examining the second of the Merseburg charms. The purpose of this incantation was to restore a broken bone or limb:

> Phol and Woden went to the forest
> Then Balder's horse sprained its foot
> Then Sinthgunt sang charms, and Sunna her sister,
> Then Friia sang charms, and Volla her sister;
> Then Woden sang charms, as he well could:
> Be it bone-sprain, be it blood-sprain, be it limb-sprain:
> Bone to bone, blood to blood,
> Limb to limb, so they glued together[19]

This is of course nothing other than an earlier version of the same troll formula we found among one of our previous examples. Yet here we instead see how pre-Christian cultic deities are the

---

19 Translated by John Lindow in *Norse Mythology: A Guide to Gods, Heroes, Rituals, and Beliefs* (Oxford: Oxford University Press, 2001), p. 227.

protagonists, with Woden/Odin himself taking on the same role Jesus had in the later charm. The main narrative, however, remains the same, and the ending lines of 'bone to bone, blood to blood, limb to limb' are identical to the early modern Swedish example quoted above.[20] In other words, in the later charm the mythic characters have been changed to other powerful entities who are more aligned with the contemporary religious context. Again, however, we should not become blinded and believe that we have here something of a heathen practice 'smuggled' into a Christian world, and that the individuals who made use of these charms were somehow trying to preserve pre-Christian religion. I would instead argue that it is the great utility of the charm as a healing method that must be the main reason for it to be preserved. Both Odin and Jesus were at various periods perceived as holding power to heal by supernatural power, therefore they can both be used as protagonists within the narrative. Likewise, Mary and her 'sisters' were highly associated with healing in a Christian world-view, and it is thus not strange that they then became the 'three maidens' who could perform the feats described in the charms.

It was noted by scholars rather early after their discovery that parts of the Merseburg charms were almost identical to other even earlier examples. Of these earlier forms the most notable is one found in the *Atharvaveda*, a collection of ancient Vedic scriptures said to have been composed between 1200-1000 BCE. This work includes many examples of magical and healing procedures and formulas, among which we find the following charm:

---

20 This specific type of narrative charm is perhaps one of the most popular in later Norse and British folk magic, and can be found in a wide variety of versions throughout northern Europe from the Middle Ages through to modern times. For a vast collection of early modern Scandinavian versions, see Ohrt, *Danmarks Trylleformler.*

Let marrow be put together with marrow,
and joint together with joint,
together what of the flesh fallen apart,
together sinew and together your bone.
Let marrow come together with marrow,
let bone grow over together with bone.
We put together your sinew with sinew,
let skin grow with skin.[21]

The similarities between this and the previous examples are striking; the mind boggles when speculating on how far back we can trace the origins of this formula, as it certainly seems to have been spread widely among the ancient Indo-Europeans. A Gaelic charm recorded in the late 19th century similarly follows the very same formula, indicating its popularity among a variety of cultural contexts:

Christ went forth
In the early morn
And found the horses' legs
Broken across.
He put bone to bone.
Sinew to sinew,
Flesh to flesh.
And skin to skin;
And as He healed that,
May I heal this.[22]

---

21 *Atharvaveda* 4.15, Paippalada Edition, quoted in Frits Staal, *Discovering the Vedas: Origins, Mantras, Rituals, Insights* (New Delhi: Penguin Books India Pvt Ltd, 2009), pp. 137-139.

22 Alexander Macbain, 'Gaelic Incantation', *Transactions of the Gaelic Society of Inverness* (1892), 17:224.

We also find the following charms documented in Devonshire and Scotland respectively:

> As Christ was riding over Mercy Bridge,
> His horse fell down and broke its leg
> He uttered these words and said;
> Bone to bone
> Sane to Sane
> Soon he was well and whole again
> In the name of the Trinity[23]

> Our Lord in hunting red,
> His sooll soot and seld;
> Donn he lighted,
> His sool sot righted'
> Blod to blod, Shenew to shenew
> To the other sent in God's name,
> In the name of the Father, Son and Holy Ghost[24]

Although this particular example is more than fascinating, we should note that we lack a narrative in the Vedic version of the charm, only what I previously referred to as a charm proper.[25] However, we do not have to look far in the *Atharvaveda* itself to find examples of narrative charms, albeit not containing the same frame-stories as those we find in Europe:

---

23 Devonshire Association Folk-lore Transactions 1862-1928, quoted in Graham King, *The British Book of Spells and Charms* (London: Troy Books, 2016), p. 115.

24 John Graham Dalyell, *The Darker Superstitions of Scotland*, quoted by A.D. Mercer in *The Wicked Shall Decay: Charms, Spell & Witchcraft of Old Britain* (California: Three Hands Press, 2018), p. 29.

25 This link was already established by Macbain in 'Gaelic Incantation'.

A charm to make a poisoned arrow harmless
The Brāhman first was brought to life ten-headed
and with faces ten.
First drinker of the Soma, he made poison ineffectual.
Far as the heavens and earth are spread in compass, far
as the Seven Rivers are extended,
So far my spell, the antidote of poison,
have I spoken hence,
The strong-winged Bird Garutmān first of all,
O Poison fed on thee:

Thou didst not gripe or make him drunk:
aye, thou becamest food for him.
Whoever with five fingers hath discharged thee
from the crooked bow,
I from the shaft have charmed away the poison
of the fastening band [...][26]

This charm continues to further describe how the arrow of
the utterer's enemy will be made harmless. The mythical narrative
explains how the Vedic god Brāhma, as well as the legendary
Garuda bird that kills snakes, subdues the power of poison. The
narrator tells of their actions and their power in conjunction with
his own motive, establishing an implicit link between the two. In
this sense, we can see once again the use of narrative in a magical
charm, as it is the very action of the mythical protagonists that
are in focus. Actually, we could perhaps affirm this as one of the
most fundamental aspects of these kinds of charms: that they seek
to infuse the magical formula with a specific type of *action* which

---

26 Ralph T.H. Griffith, *Hymns of the Atharva Veda* (1895), <https://www.
sacred-texts.com/hin/av/index.htm>.

is performed by a powerful entity. Here one does not call on the gods or saints in the hope they will perform a specific action (as in an invocation, prayer, or conjuration), but instead directly recounts the acts they have either performed in a mythical past, or at least such actions as are compatible with their nature.

Perhaps the most clear example of this form of action among narrative charms is the way in which a powerful entity meets a malign entity whom it then drives off. We saw an example of such a charm in a narrative troll formula quoted in the first chapter, yet its origins can be traced even further back in time. In his essay *The Mermaid and the Devil's Grandmother*, A. A. Barb recounts an ancient Roman charm from the 3rd century CE as the following:

Against Migraine

Antaura came out from the sea. She shouted aloud like a
hind, she cried out like a cow. Artemis of Ephesos comes
to meet her. 'Antaura, where are you bringing the half-
head-pain? Not to…?'[27]

The scroll on which the charm was written is damaged and unfortunately we cannot read the rest, yet Barb fills in the blank by quoting another charm. This one, however, was found in a later medieval Italian manuscript, and instead of having the goddess Artemis as its heroine it has Jesus in her place:

Migraine-prayer against the headache

Migraine came out from the sea rioting and roaring, and
our Lord Jesus came to meet it and said to it:
'Where are you bringing headache and pain in the skull

---

27 A.A. Barb, 'Antaura. The Mermaid and the Devil's Grandmother: A Lecture', *Journal of the Warburg and Courtauld Institutes*, 29 (1966), 2.

and in the eyes and inflammation and tears dizziness?'
And the Headache answered to our Lord Jesus Christ:
We are going to sit down in the head of the servant of
God So-and-So.
And our Lord Jesus Christ tells it:
'Look here, do not go into my servant, but be off
altogether and go into the wild mountains and settle in a
bull's head. There you may eat flesh, there drink blood,
there ruin the eyes, there darken the head, wriggle. But
if you do not obey me I shall destroy you there on the
burning mountain where no dog barks and the cock does
not crow. You who have set a limit to the sea stop the
headache and migraine and the pain in the skull and
between the eyes and on the lids and from the marrow
from the servant of the Lord So-and-So.'[28]

Barb connects the personified migraine found in these charms
with even older material and concludes that its origins lie in the
ancient Middle East. The demonic *Antaura* which we meet in
the first version is, according to Barb, none other than one of
the evil spirits we meet among the Babylonians and Assyrians in
the form of *Lamashtu* and *Lilith*. Again, this is perhaps of interest
in a purely historical sense, but what is most striking is how the
actual narrative has come to survive over such a long period of
time. The characters might change, but the main power of the
narrative and the actions performed by the protagonist remain the
same: if a benevolent and protective saint or deity has the power
to command a lesser malign entity, this force can be utilized in a
great number of ways. In the early modern Scandinavian version
that I initially quoted, Jesus is able to ward off a personification

---

28 Barb, 'Antaura', 2.

of envy which has afflicted someone with the evil eye. There are numerous examples of other personified ills which other charms are aimed at diverting and, as we have seen, migraine can be one of them. It is not strange, then, that we find this type of charm so popular and widely used throughout history, as it can be applied to basically any kind of illness or threat just by adjusting it slightly to the given situation.

The ancient Egyptians made immense use of mythic motives and narratives in their magical and religious practice, conceiving of the art of magic as directly linked to the divine power of utterance and script.[29] Yet, although there is a plethora of examples to be found where magicians used narratives drawn directly from well-known mythological sources, we still find examples of *historiolae* where the 'source' remains somewhat obscure. For example, an Egyptian charm for bird-catching reads:

> Horus, son of Isis, ascended a hill in order to sleep. He sang his melodies, spread his nets, caught a falcon, a bank-bird, a mountain pelican.[30]

There are no references to any well-known mythological story to be found here, and one is tempted to believe that the reason why the god Horus has been chosen as the protagonist is merely due to his connection with birds (especially the falcon). One could speculate whether this particular charm is derived from a non-scribal context, one in which the author did not have access to proper textual cultic myths and instead had to 'make do' with

29 Robert K. Ritner, The Mechanics of Ancient Egyptian Magical Practice, Series: Studies in Ancient Oriental Civilizations, 54 (Chicago: Oriental Institute, 1993), p. 35.

30 L. Kákosy, 'Remarks on the Interpretation of a Coptic Magical Text', *Acta Orientalia*, 13 (1961), 325-28.

the analogies he or she saw fit for the purpose at hand. What is interesting, though, is that we find here a 'myth' whose only, or at least original, function was that of magical application.[31]

This raises the question of whether these kinds of narratives must have a foundation in a generic myth or not, since as we have seen it is sometimes rather difficult to connect them directly with popular or well-known mythical motifs. We will rarely find Jesus riding over bridges or Mary binding snakes in the Bible, nor will we find any mention in Greco-Roman mythology of how the goddess Artemis caused migraine to return to the sea, for that matter. What we do find, however, is that in certain cultures and during certain periods of time, some people understood all of these figures to have the power to ward off certain types of illnesses and to heal. The narratives are, in this sense, plausible scenarios in which this power is put into action. These can be directly drawn from well-known mythical stories and motifs such as the Vedic charms quoted above, but sometimes this is not needed and it is only the inventiveness and imagination of the magician which seem to set the limits. An example of a direct infusion of a myth into a charm is a Jewish love spell found among the *Greek Magical Papyri* where the magician is to equate physical sulfur with that which rained over Sodom and Gomorrah in the Book of Genesis, in order make the heart of a specific victim burn with passion.

Love spell of attraction,
fire divination over unburnt sulfur, thus: Take seven
lumps of unburnt sulfur and make an altar fire from
vine wood. Say this spell over the lumps one by one and
throw them into the fire.

---

31 David Frankfurter, 'Narrating Power: The theory and practice of the magical historiola in ritual spells', in P. Mirecki & M. Meyer (eds), *Ancient Magic and Ritual Power* (Netherlands: Brill, 1995) pp. 472-73.

This is the spell: "The heavens of heavens opened, and the angels of God descended and overturned the five / cities of Sodom and Gomorrah, Admah, Zeboiim, and Segor. A woman who heard the voice became a pillar of salt. You are the sulfur which God rained down on the middle of Sodom and Gomorrah, Admah, Zeboiim, and Segor; you are the sulfur which served God – so also serve me, NN, in regards to her, NN / and do not allow her to go to bed or to find sleep until she comes and fulfills the mystery rite of Aphrodite"
[...][32]

Here the mythological link is direct, as the magician seeks to draw on the same essential fiery force God used when the ancient cities were destroyed in biblical times as that which should be present in the heart of his victim. The myth used here is an already established one, and we can most probably assume that the charm was constructed when the magician sought out an already defined instance where a specific divine power was at work for the purpose of 'tapping into it' in a ritual context. If we think of it purely as an analogy it seems a bit strange: the sulfur that fell over Sodom and Gomorrah did not merely heat them up, but completely *annihilated* the cities. Yet from the perspective of intensity and force, this is a grand source of power to make use of if one is after a profound effect of passion. The magician could have resorted to drawing this power from the fire of his own hearth, but would that have the same 'bite' in comparison to the scourge of God himself consuming cities in flames? It is also interesting to note that these cities were destroyed due to the sinful

32 PGM XXXVI. 295-311 in Hans Dieter Betz, *The Greek Magical Papyri in Translation: Including the Demotic Spells,* Volume 1 Texts (Chicago: University of Chicago Press, 1996), p. 276.

sexual appetites of their inhabitants, which present us with yet another source of power to be utilized by the magical working. It establishes a further dimension to the charm, where two aspects of fiery lust and passion appear on the same stage, which sets the tone for what the magician has set out to accomplish. Likewise, the reference to Lot's wife, who was turned to a pillar of salt whilst gazing back at the burning Sodom, might also be a means of establishing a form of binding or paralyzing effect on the target. Thus, although we find here a fully established mythical narrative in use, it is still utilized in a highly inventive, dynamic, and multi-dimensional manner. Indeed, there is a certain type of poetic and evocative play with thematic elements at work here, amplifying the spell in a manner which follows a sort of twilight logic; the use of this particular myth, for this particular end, lends its meaning to a paradoxical yet intuitive meaning that must have been clear for the narrator, but is more ambiguous to an outsider too caught up in how the myth is normally understood.

It is not my intention to try to fully 'decipher' the origins of these mythical scenarios, nor to locate them in an exact historical context; I merely want to highlight that the use of narratives in these charms is highly nuanced and complex, and that they do not always follow a form which is 'logical' to the outsider. Although some of the specific 'stories' can remain highly intact over centuries (or even millennia), their content and form are still rather fluid and can be adjusted to both context and the purpose at hand. In one way, this is how humans have always dealt with stories and myths of any sort – they are constantly re-configured and re-interpreted in order to remain relatable. Of course, the *historiolae* are, as previously noted, never produced either to entertain or explain anything – they are instead used in a context where they are perceived as having the magical ability to *directly* heal, harm, and so on. They appear to work on an intuitive 'gut' level, caught up in webs of meaning which only make sense from the inside. To understand them we must therefore locate them in their correct context, which is a magical/ritualistic one, and see how they can be perceived to function within it.

The use of so-called barbarous names *(onomata barbara)* and other 'nonsensical' words and figures is a well-known feature in most magical traditions. With these, the magician never needs to literally 'understand' the words, but still makes use of them.[33] This has sometimes led skeptics to conclude that magic mainly deals with completely illogical and naïve methodology, since it draws on what is often found to be nonsensical material. We must instead come to terms with the idea that the magician always understands the barbarous names, albeit perhaps not in a common literal sense. Their meaning is instead drawn from their context, their purpose, and their functionality, and can be informed via a myriad of factors such as the circumstances by which they were first discovered by the magician (such as if the material was found in an authoritative text or handed down from a teacher), or the manifold results the magician obtains when putting the words into practice. Although tradition and the general cultural context are highly important when it comes to meaning, the subjective dimension is perhaps even more vital and is highly tied to the practicality of the formula used. The magical tradition becomes embodied in the sole practitioner, who shapes it according to his world-view and practice, formulating meaning in methods through the lived experience of ritual action. The individual practitioner must thus

---

33 The great late antique theurgist and philosopher Iamblichus proposed these *logae* to only be intelligible to daimons and other super-terrestrial intelligences. Still, as I argue here, one could likewise propose that their meaning could be found within their functionality as a means of esoteric communication and thus that they are indeed meaningful to the theurgist, albeit not in a common lexical sense.

establish a meaning for the charms himself, not merely through intellectual speculation and literal interpretation, but rather though experiential experimentation. There must be an established connection and certainty in the magician of the clear purpose of a spell or a word of power, since otherwise it will lack the force to cause an effect.

To do this, one needs to 'access' the narrative of the charm and its underlying functionality: for instance, one will need to contemplate the relationship between figures such as Jesus and a demonic entity causing migraine and how it plays out in the *historiolae*. The general religious context will inform us that Jesus is a divine figure who can drive out demons, which would naturally include migraine. Now, if these two figures were to meet, the Son of God would logically be able to ward off the ill-willed headache. This meaning is brought forth and actualized via the narrative, repeated by the magician who himself is completely sure of the unfolding event and the connotations of the meeting between the two entities. Yet this is merely on a theoretical level; the real meaning of this event is displayed when it is applied to a real-world situation. The narrative and its inner dynamics are then instantiated and defined via effect – otherwise it remains but a story or a hypothetical example. The meaning of the story is, in this sense, that it is not a story at all, but rather that it is a direct and lived reality. It is an evocation of a particular act of power by a great spiritual force, instantiated for the purpose of having a specified causal effect.

To the ancient Indian ritualist, there must have been little discussion about whether Brāhma could or could not save one from poisoning, as the *Vedas* informed him that the god has this ability.[34] As this ability is perceived as unmistakably real, it can then be 'tapped into' and applied by certain means, just as any natural force, such as the physical elements, can be harnessed by man for his own ends. In this way, we quickly see that we are no longer in the territory of 'myth' as it is commonly perceived in secular society, where myths are at best able to inspire with food for thought, or create some type of emotional response. Their 'reality' is located in a distant and dim past or otherworld which one can only connect to in an indirect sense via interpretation. They are fantastic fictions which need to be processed and/or analyzed via our frame of reference in order to have an effect. To the magician, on the other hand, these tales do not belong to an ancient past, but rather are structural scenarios which can be accessed at any time or place. The magician is someone who can truly bring the myths to life in the expression's fullest sense – he or she is a story-teller whose stories are truths of power and action. What matters in this case is not intellectual understanding so much as a direct and lived connection with the principles and beings mentioned in the charms. The ritualistic narrator has access to that which many of us who live in a modern, secularized society believe to be simply dreams or fantasy.

In his work on myth in connection to magic, Mircea Eliade argues that ritualists can make use of cosmogonic powers described in mythic images and hymns in order to bridge the gap between the two realms of the sacred and the profane.[35] Eliade presents an

---

34 The later philosophical and philological stream of Vedic exegesis known as Mīmāṃsā commonly asserts that the *Vedas* are to be regarded as revealed, timeless truth. Although this particular school of thought also has 'atheistic' strands, it still fundamentally proposes the absolute infallible nature of the scriptures.

35 Mircea Eliade, *Myth and Reality*, tr. Willard R. Trask (New York: Harper & Row, 1963), p. 25.

example where an Asian healer creates a cosmic mandala on the floor in order to heal an ill patient, and explains that this is a procedure to more or less bring the ancient past back into the contemporary space, where 'the patient is immersed in the primordial fullness of life; he is penetrated by the gigantic forces that, *in illo tempore* (the ancient mythic past), made the Creation possible.'[36]

Eliade has understood something vital here, yet unfortunately misses a crucial point by being caught up in a temporal perspective. In fact, to the magician, there is no such thing as an 'otherworld' which stands in conflict with what we could call a 'conventional' world at all, and there is no explicit distance in regards to a temporal setting between them. The power formulated in the mandala or the cosmological myth is ever-present at all times; it is a matter of it being actualized and applied by means of its depiction or recitation. To a person who constantly lives within a 'sacred space', there cannot be any such thing as the 'profane', or, at the least, the lines between the two worlds are permanently blurred. Instead what is needed is a methodology and philosophy that can organize and specify a practical modality for the magician to deal with the world in a 'sacred' manner. It matters little what both current academics and occultists are fetishizing as a so-called 'otherness' here; in pure practical terms the magician is not interested in upholding a distance to the 'other', but the absolute opposite when transcending the imagined duality between the

---

36 Eliade, *Myth and Reality*, p. 25

domains of spirit and matter.[37] What is found in these practices are methods of intensification of highly specified notions of power to fill various functions (such as healing, harming, etc.). We could perhaps also say that as the stories actually take place in 'mythical space', or 'out of time', they are made paradoxically even easier to access in any given situation. As they are not clearly reducible to common spatio-temporal limitations, they can take place anytime and anywhere, which gives them a great dynamic advantage. But this still does not make them potential reoccurrences of things past; it rather affirms their accessibility in the present and makes them even less 'other' and even more tangible and intensified, albeit in a highly subtle sense.[38]

At first glance the *historiolae* seem to take place in the past: they are usually written in the past tense and tell of happenings of ancient heroes or divine agents in pre-history. It could then be convenient to assume that they are merely functioning as a type of

---

37 Likewise, a similar view can be applied to the so-called 'barbaric names' of ancient and medieval magic. Their function is not merely to impress a more esoteric glamor onto the magical operation, nor to widen the gap between the sacred and profane aspects of reality, but rather to cut straight through them. The formulas give the sorcerer direct access to a cosmic force or domain which is not accessible in 'normal' lexical terms. As a practitioner of both Scandinavian folk magic and traditional Shakta Tantra, wherein mantric practices are fundamental, I am usually highly hesitant to draw any direct parallels between Eastern and Western methodology, but this is an area where there seems to be a slight theoretical overlap between the two, especially in comparing the use of the seven vowels within ancient theurgy and the so-called Seed-syllable mantras.

38 I would argue that there are still examples where a certain form of the concept of 'otherness' is at play within some *historiolae*, and will return to this when discussing what could be called their internal geography and locality. However, this is quite a different matter and should not be confused with the general metaphysics of the charms.

'echo' of ancient happenings, where the magician seeks to ritually 're-enact' a previous action of healing or harming. The use of stories drawn from mythic narratives would, by this line of thinking, give authority to the sorcerer, which is thought to either liken their own action to that of the powerful being which performed it with success *in illo tempore*, or even to help the sorcerer to identify with the being. By stating that 'once upon a time, X performed Y', the magician, by means of some form of ritualistic authority, can by extension claim 'likewise I can perform Y'. Although this line of reasoning is not too foreign to some methods of magic and mystical practice, I think it would be an oversimplification to consider it the fundamental idea present in the utterance of all forms of narrative charms. When we recite a story, even though it is in the past tense, the emotional impact of it is still a matter which happens in the present. This is because we have the ability to *relate* to the story, to cognitively envision it and empathetically feel for the characters in it. Yet although the feelings stirred up can be cognitively tangible, present, and fully real, the context usually tells us that this is but a response to a fictional event, and we are thus safe to view it as distant. The stories of the *historiolae* completely cut through such barriers and instead essentially assume the presence and reality of their characters as well as their happenings. Uttering such a story will likewise not only enable an emotional response, but a direct activation of whatever forces are at work in it. It is, then, highly important that this scenario actually plays out in a complete and final sense. The action is fulfilled, finalized, and concluded to its end, and not simply left open to interpretation. It is not enough to simply grab a hammer in one hand and a nail in the other if the purpose is to build a house. Formulating the stories in the past tense and drawing them to a completed conclusion gives the charms a more defined intensity, paradoxically making them more functional in a present situation.

It is interesting that we can even find examples of *historiolae* where the appearance of a 'mythical past' and a present situation are completely switched. For example, an ancient Sumerian incantation for the treatment of illness inflicted by demonic influence reads:

> The evil Ugud-demon, inflecting the quiet street, comes
>   from a hidden place, overwhelming thoroughfare.
>   …The Dimme and Dima-demons who spatter the
> victim, internal disease and stricture, sickness, headache,
>   and the Ala-demon covering the patient,
>   (all) agitated the distraught man like a storm and
>   sprinkled him with gall.
>   The patient will progressively lose his vitality,
>   undulating [like a wave,]
>   [he will neither be able to dine]nor[drink].
> Asalluhi took note, and entered the temple, to his father
>   Ea, saying
> {here Asalluhi repeats the events, ending with the plea:}
>   'I do not kno[w what] I should do about it;
>   what can relieve him?'.
>   [Ea]answers his son Asalluhi:
>   'My son, what do you not know,
>   and what could I add to it?
> …Whatever I know, you also know. Go, my son, Asalluhi,
>   {a ritual prescription follows; the concluding section
> starts with a command to the demons:} Be adjured [by
>   the] great gods, so that you depart…[39]

---

39 UHF VII/647-89 translated by Markham Geller, quoted in Seth L. Sanders, et al., 'A Historiography of Demons: Preterit-thema, Para-myth, and Historiola in the Morphology of Genres', *Historiography in the Cuneiform World* (Bethesda: CDL Press, 2001), pp. 429-440.

In this charm it is notable that the patient has first become afflicted by the demons, and that the gods (Ea and his son Asalluhi) discuss the treatment and ritual expulsion of the demonic influences after this has taken place. So although it is written in a general past tense, it places the action of the deities not in a mythic past, but rather closer to the present than the time that the patient became ill. Jumping a few millennia forward, we can see the same structure at work in the following Swedish troll formula:

> The Virgin Mary went down the road and cried;
> then she met Jesus –
> Why are you crying?
> – My cow is bereft of fortitude even to his liver and lung,
> to his teeth and his tongue; can you heal her?
> Oh yes, with malt and with salt and valerian root shall
> your cow be healed, in the name of God the Father and
> of the Son and of the Holy Ghost.
> [Recite over cattle feed, salt and valerian three times,
> when the cow has been robbed of its fortitude][40]

This explicitly highlights how dynamic and fluid the perception of temporality can be among the *historiolae*, and confirms that we should not confuse stories of gods and the saints in general with events *in illo tempore*. Rather, we here find a view which affirms that their concerns and reality are not detached from those within the world of the living, but are firmly connected with it. Indeed, their practices are directly aligned with those of the healer and the magician in the present moment, where their actions overlap in a unified effort to cure the patient (or the cow as in the latter example).

---

40 Johnson, *Svartkonstböcker*, p. 322.

Taking a further look at our historical material, we do not even have to propose that these charms have taken influence from the realm of the 'supernatural'. An ancient Greco-Roman narrative charm to produce good digestion reads as follows:

> A wolf went along road, along track.
> Raw food he devoured, liquids he drank[41]

In this charm we find no mythical material whatsoever. Its simplicity is almost baffling, drawing merely on the notion that wolves have a great appetite (we all know the expression 'hungry like a wolf') and can even eat raw flesh without causing problems for their digestion. So, here we notice that we can do without any mythological scenario, since all we need is a scenario which, in one way or another, contains a fulfilled action. This particular action is meaningful from a purely naturalistic and empirical perspective, rather than being from a more complex theological or mythological one, and does not take place in a remote, distant past, but could theoretically have taken place just a minute ago in some woodland close by. Still, both charms are in theory made to function in a similar magical fashion. It is thus not at all strange to think that we are dealing with pure analogy here, or a *similis similibus*; namely that the narrator wishes to say 'as X, so Y'. As previously noted, this is indeed the route that the likes of Frazer took when categorizing similar practices as sympathetic magic. My main point is, however, that if we examine the properties at play within the *historiolae* from the perspective of a magical context, we discover that what is sought out is not a linkage in a vague and abstract sense, but rather a method of harnessing the *same* force which functions within one

---

41 Hein 85, quoted in H.S. Versnel, 'The poetics of the magical charm: an essay in the words of power', in *Magic in the Ancient World*, ed. by P. Mirecki & M. Meyer (Netherlands: Brill, 2001), p. 123.

exemplified scenario in a given situation. The hunger and the
means of digestion, which the wolf displays in the charm quoted
above, are also set out to be established in the client seeking the
magician's help to process food and liquid. This could be thought
of as analogy, or sympathy, to the extent that the narrative functions
as a spectrum to locate this principle in action. Yet ultimately this
is not so much a matter of resemblance or reference, as that of
transference and application.

A rare, yet highly interesting example of how power can be
drawn and utilized via charms can be found in a Swedish herding
call documented in the 19th century. The song is said to have been
initially sung by a giant in order to lure the cattle that belonged to
a herder into his home in the mountains.

> Du Hihi Hangela, Borsta Rangela, Läggete Hari, Du
> I våperans Kari, Du Röjte. Sköjte, Räcke, Smäcke,
> Långtfrå! Kom Ole, Bås E' kämpehack,
> Kom Sjölabrand!
> Och Locke fram mera Till mor i hål! Kom ko, kom kalf,
> kom tjura, Och sede underli' djura!
> Kom Socke-Thore Och Skiversman!
> Kom Socke-Thore Och Stiversman!
> Så kom der Socke-Thore lång, Med hammar' och tång,
> Och satte sitt märke på stoltanhorn; Det vållte den
> Berggubbe skallut[42]

The song begins with the giant calling the cows by their
names, establishing his power over them. The being then conjures
the heathen god Thor, who via the advent of Christianity is now

---

42 Sverker Ek, *Bohuslänska Vallvisor in Bohuslänska Folkminnen: Studier och
Upptäckningar* (Uddevalla: Hallmans Boktryckeri A., 1922) pp. 38-39.

paradoxically seen as the ruler and protector of giants, rather than their enemy. Thor is called on as a smith, and the mountain-dwelling giant asks him to put his mark (a lightning bolt?) on the cows, in order to claim them for himself. However, to make things even more enigmatic, the final line of the song tells us that this very action actually causes the giant's death – Thor crushes its skull with his hammer. To understand how this song was thought to function, we are told that traditionally it was only to be sung in times of great danger, when the herd was lost and it was suspected that they had been stolen by giants or trolls.[43] What we see then is that the power of the song and the invocation of the heathen god, originally thought to be sung by the giant, has here been reversed and claimed by the herder. By reciting the song, which uncovers the misdeeds and evil intentions of the one who first sang it, the herder himself daringly calls upon Thor to punish the thief. This example again shows us the fluidity of how narrative can function in charms, as even a 'negative' or harmful story can become protective when applied under the right circumstances.

I would propose that many of the misunderstandings found within previous academic scholarship regarding the narrative charms were based on scholars' disregard of the means, methods, and circumstances in which they were recited. Even among scholars who emphasize a performative dimension at play within the internal logic of these verbal devices, they are usually only thought to function on a symbolic or analogical level. What I have instead hoped to show in this chapter is that from a practical standpoint, emphasis is always to be found in the notion of living power and how it is applied. If this is not made clear, it is very easy to fall into the trap of conceiving of these charms as either bad fairytales or primitive and misdirected logic. If the charms are only approached

---

43 Ek, *Bohuslänska Vallvisor in Bohuslänska Folkminnen*, p. 41.

from a linguistic perspective, the actual metaphysical aspects of the process are not taken into account and the conclusion will thus be lacking. In the following chapters I will try to further elaborate on this, showing how the practical dimensions that are in place in the performance of these charms must first be taken into account in order to for us to examine them theoretically.

THE APPLICATION OF THE NARRATIVE CHARMS

The troll formulas in traditional Norse folk magic are more or less always spoken, but usually never out loud.[44] This is because they are thought to lose their power if known by another person, and are therefore mostly perceived as well-hidden secrets, carefully protected from outsiders.[45] There are various techniques for their utterance, which Johannes Gårdbäck summarises as follows:

> It may be spoken out loud in a commanding voice or it may be spoken with the breath held and teeth clenched tight, after which the breath is blown toward or into the target. The held-breath method is more common when the spell is said over materials or in physical contact with a patient. The two methods may be combined, for instance when the first part of a narrative formula is read aloud but the speech of a powerful entity is recited with the breath held and the breath is blown upon the target.[46]

---

44 Gårdbäck, *Trolldom*, p. 72.

45 In Norwegian the charms are known as runes (Norwegian *runa/ runer*), which puts emphasis on their esoteric nature. This also gives room for speculation with regard to the ancient magical practices related to the runes mentioned within the Eddic corpus. Modern day neo-pagan reconstructions of ancient Norse magic seem to put a major emphasis on the written aspect of the runes, while in actuality the oral practice of charms seem to have been equally important in ancient times.

46 Gårdbäck, *Trolldom*, p. 72.

As we can see, there are variations in the performance of the charms, yet they are in part always kept secret from other individuals. When the charm was spoken out loud, it was either not in the physical presence of another person or, if another person was present, they would only have been able to hear the initial part of the narrative.[47] The method of 'whispering' the incantation or charm is reminiscent of the practices we find in Russian folk magic.[48] The whispering technique also has the advantage of accessing the charm in a more concrete and physical manner, where the breath uttering the spell can be blown in a specific direction. For example, the breath is commonly blown into a glass of water or alcohol, which is then drunk by the client or applied to an object.[49] The magical force is thus transferred from the mind and mouth of the magician into a specific target which is imbued with its healing or harming power. Even if spoken out loud, the words must be directed and spoken 'over', 'unto', or 'into' a specified target, which could either be physically present or absent.

From here we can begin to discern an idea that words in and of themselves can be imbued with power, whether they are actually heard or not. The utterance, albeit in a whisper, functions

47 It is notable that cunning men or women would recite the initial part of a narrative charm out loud. I will return to this matter in chapter four when discussing my own understanding of the inner dynamics of these charms, especially in relation to their use of 'imagination' and the setting of what could be termed ritual space.

48 Joseph L. Conrad, 'Russian Ritual Incantations: Tradition, Diversity and Continuity', *The Slavic and East European Journal*, 33:3 (1989), 425.

49 A further example of this sort of technique might be the practice of physically consuming ink which has been used to write spells, found within both common medieval Jewish and Christian folk magic where the ink of biblical psalms was drunk, as well as ritual consumption of written angelic/demonic names in, for instance, the *Ars Notoria*. See Davies, *Grimoires: A History of Magic Books*, pp. 4-5.

as a manifestation of a movement in the mind of the magician, formulized via the sentences or words. Just like when we think of something, and then express it in words to another person, we extract the abstract thought and formulate it as physical sound, moving it from a state of being invisible and private to the realm of physicality and outwards action. In one way, there is nothing 'magical' about this whatsoever, as we constantly move in-between these realms of reality in our daily lives without seeing something especially extraordinary about it. The main difference is, however, that within magical practice one makes use of a perspective in which the line between these two realms is perceived to be much more blurred than the post-Cartesian individual usually wants to admit. Within the practice of charms, the word is a direct extension or activation of subjective phenomena, directed outwards so as to establish an effect on a target. Thus, it matters little if the words spoken are actually heard by an audience, since the power which they convey is not dependent on how they might be perceived by a recipient, but rather on how they are established by the one who utters them.

Within contemporary psychoanalysis, a subjective idea, fantasy, or obsessive thought-pattern is commonly thought to have great significance for an individual's mental and physical well-being. Yet apart from having indirect effects on the surrounding world, these psychological principles are understood to be enclosed within the subject. As an individual, my thoughts and my state of mind 'belong' to myself and are contained within a private sphere which is spatially confined to the body. In my opinion, this view is built on a problematic theory of mind and questionable ontological assumptions on several levels, yet the most obvious criticism would be that as consciousness cannot fundamentally be reduced to a physical substance, it does not ultimately have to be bound to or enclosed within any one location in space. Without falling into an almost endless discussion regarding deeper metaphysics and the philosophy of mind, I would at least point out that what we find within most magical traditions is a view where such reductionist thinking is not present and where consciousness, mind, soul, and spirit claim a more dynamic nature in regard to how confined they are to spatiality. Here, subtle expressions of the mind are thought to hold power and energy, which muddle our firm common modern spirit/matter divide. Emotions or ideas can in this sense be perceived as pseudo-physical in that they can be 'attached' to physical objects. The famous conception of the evil eye, for instance, presents us with the notion that an expression of the mind (in this case, various negative emotional forces such as envy, spite, and anger) can *directly* affect another person through a mere glance. The movement of emotions, ideas, mental images, and so on is not usually perceived to be solidly spatially fixed within the confines of a single subject, but can also subtly move from one location to another, either by pure accident or by intent. Just as a physical body which functions like a host for various mental states, dreams, and longings, a word or an image can also work as a 'container' for them. The magician is thus, in many ways, a person who has mastered the art of transference of various subtle energies from one place to another, be it via the spoken word, a movement of the body, or a mere thought.[50]

---

50 Various traditions have applied different forms of philosophical conceptions and terminology to flesh out these notions which must be kept in mind when trying to formulate a type of overarching theory in secular terms. Within traditional Trolldom, for example, a human being is understood to be a unity of several principles of being, some more closely linked to the physical body than others. These principles are usually badly translated into modern psychological language, yet for convenience I have made an explicit difference between the term 'mind', which should be understood as something of a sum total of psycho-physiological processes, and 'consciousness', which is rather the fundamental mode of reality in which mind-stuff appears.

Returning to the specific procedure of working with charms, we can, for example, see how the ancient Egyptians would be able to access such power by simply pouring water over or touching an inscription of a narrative charm or a holy name.[51] This shows how the very words in and of themselves were, when 'activated', thought to bring forth a desired effect. While cautious of sounding somewhat materialistic, one could perhaps think of this as a type of machinery, coming to life by the infusion of energy. The letters are like cogwheels which are set in motion, or the arms of a windmill which turn by harnessing the force of the air. I am personally tempted to think about these *stelae* as dry tongues which, when offered water, will recite the words again, setting the narrative of the spell in motion once more.[52] Another, more organic, analogy would be to think of them as obscure images which are revealed to an observer by an act of illumination, or a forgotten dream which is suddenly remembered and comes to the forefront of one's mind. In more precise words, it is *brought into awareness*. The story told in the charm is only potential in its engraved form and is in need of being encountered and actualized. The world imbued in the words is always 'there', present by means of its formulized reality; however, it can only be utilized by the practitioner when properly expressed, observed, or 'activated'. Just like a book which stands forgotten on a shelf needs to be taken out and read for its text to

---

51 Frankfurter, 'Narrating Power: The Theory and Practice of the Magical Historiola' in *Ritual Spells*, p. 460. The charm narrated is probably that of the goddess Isis rescuing a poisoned Horus. This particular 'myth' has only come down to us in the form of a *historiola*; we could perhaps infer that this *is* the original function of the narrative, namely as a charm and not a 'story'.

52 The Tibetan use of prayer-wheels and prayer flags also comes to mind, where mantras are 'recited' via the movement of the wheel or that of the wind blowing through the flags.

be useful to us, the *historiola* is meant to be accessed by revisiting and reciting it. The water poured over the engraved charms can thus be regarded as a physical version of how the mind functions by means of awareness. By placing one's mind's eye on a specific thought, emotion, or mental vision, it is brought to our attention and can be interacted with and expressed. The charm establishes a complete scenario (usually) involving grand spiritual agents, meaning that the potential present in the words is intentionally produced to create a specific form of interaction. This process, compared to more 'mundane' types of interaction, is of course highly specialized and 'esoteric', as the principles expressed in the words are perceived as living and powerful entities. Their reality and their actions are made available through the awareness and experience of the subject, whose consciousness acts like a stage on which the story plays out. The words pronounce the structure or flow of this action – they are the script, so to speak, and are thus the link between the subject and the powers they seek to interact with.

All this could be described as a form of revitalization or animation of properties which are latent and waiting to be acted out. The water poured upon the stele, like the living energy of one's awareness, quickens the actions of the characters and enables one to participate in their movement. Again, this is mostly a matter of uncovering experiential meaning and the ability of the practitioner to connect with the power to be worked with. Yet we still often find examples of practices where this direct subjective link is rather vague, and one mainly relies on a more general idea of how the practice works. For instance, we can see this in the method of the Egyptian stele described above, which could be used by anyone who at least knew that intentionally pouring water over it would result in a certain type of effect. The notion here is most likely that the words in and of themselves were thought to hold certain powers. We find this sort of idea in various forms scattered across several cultures, and it can unfortunately not be dealt with here in any depth; however, it should be noted that we do find similar assumptions in regard to the charms and more typical forms of *nomina barbara* and so on. The charms, though, are rather units of words which together function in a very similar manner. Usually, within the Trolldom tradition, the formulas are not merely recited once within a ritual setting, but can be repeated several times until they give the desired effect. This first of all shows that we are dealing with a highly organic form of practice which does not claim to function 'mechanically' in any way. Secondly, this reveals how close the *historiolae* are perceived to be in practical likeness to other, more condensed magical formulae that do not involve narratives of any sort. Yet even if they both might be considered vehicles of power in and of themselves, the practice of 'charging' or animating them, via mental or physical stimuli, still seems to be a common trait for *voces magicae* and narrative charms alike.

If we return to the notion that the energy expressed through words can be 'placed' within a physical object, it brings us to the art of constructing a talisman or amulet. Words and images of power, such as a *historiola*, can in this practice be both uttered as well as inscribed onto the chosen parchment or artefact, which then functions as a container for it. The examples of such practices are so widespread that it would be somewhat excessive to go into detail here, but it should not be too far-fetched to draw a parallel between the mythic narrative used in the *historiolae* and amulets inscribed with mythic scenarios such as Saint George slaying the dragon, or even the crucifixion of Jesus. The mere depiction of the mythic scene can be understood to contain principles which can be accessed by magical means as it formulates a precise display of power. The image of a saint, hero, or deity in action provides us with a potential for a magical effect as it establishes their agency before our very eyes. Yet as with the spoken charm, this action has to be well established via the magician and imbued with the proper connection to the source of this agency. This can be done by drawing or inscribing the object with the image as well as uttering the *historiola* into it, so as to fully 'charge' the amulet with the right influence drawn from a direct bond with the spiritual being in question. Various other forms of occult methods, such as application of suitable *materia magica* and inscription of esoteric names or *charaktêres*, as well as the observance of astrological timings and so forth, might also be taken into account here as they can be thought to bring similar types of empowerments to the object as well.

The connection between the visual depiction of a specific mythical scene and the *historiola* should not be underestimated, because it tells us something essential about the cognitive dimension at work in these magical methods. The stories used in the charms can be thought of as visual procedures or scenarios of images set in motion, performed through the process of words constructed as a narrative. Obviously this does not mean that they need to be clearly visualized, but rather that they verbally formulate an 'imaginative' event which can also be expressed in images. The charms are neither abstract nor even nonsensical in a linguistic sense and are clearly depicting a happening which can theoretically be envisioned to take place. This gives them both a certain element of clarity or even 'solidity', as well as flexibility in terms of mediation.

Still, we should be careful not to believe that we can reduce the potency of the incantations to either a series of words or a set of images – it is the energies which are expressed with the words or images that essentially count. These energies are defined and formulated via verbal, textual, and visual media which function as containers or 'bodies' for them. To the experienced practitioner it does not matter in what shape or form these media are expressed, be they rigorously apparent in an objective sense or not, as long as the link between the source of energy and the media is made subconsciously and subjectively clear. A mere muttering of the *historiolae* or a scribble of an angel holding a sword can be sufficient for the experienced practitioner. Not much thought or complicated mental exercise has to go into it, since the words or images are already 'charged' in the mind of the magician and can simply be applied directly to various circumstances without any excessive ritualistic jargon. To use linguistic terms, the referent has been established subjectively and as it does not need to be communicated to another subject in a 'conventional' lexical sense, it can be referred to in whatever manner is most effective for the sorcerer. It is, however, worth repeating that this does not mean that the expression (i.e. the charm, figure, name, etc.) is ultimately arbitrary or an ad hoc affair; usually the opposite is true. Magic is commonly highly dependent on a firm acknowledgment of tradition and transference of power, where certain forms of expressions are many times viewed as 'intrinsically' effective. Still, the mastery and methodological utilization of these expressions are dependent on how well the sorcerer can function as a medium for the underlying principles that are depicted. This matter is fundamentally tied to the skill and performative knowledge of the practitioner. New levels of insight and technique should then be expected, and this might then lead to innovations and personal developments within a given tradition. The power attained via this personalized connection with the charm and its esoteric properties is essentially regarded as a well-guarded secret from outsiders, sometimes only passed on via ritualistic procedures incorporating various 'buffers' so that the transference from one practitioner to the other may keep its force wholly intact. If, on the other hand, the charm is spoken clearly out loud, this power is subsequently perceived as being drained, as it can no longer function as a solid container to hold it. Even translating a charm to another language, or changing its form significantly, might disrupt and drain it of the energy which the tradition has invested into it, as the words in and of themselves (including the pronunciation and so on) have formally become the vehicles of the magical force.[53]

The charms are often uttered in conjunction with the performance of specific actions, such as ritual binding, application of remedies, and so on. The *historiola* adds yet another layer to these actions, establishing a unified whole where the additional procedures are embedded. We see this clearly in those charms which explicitly mention the actions that are to be undertaken along with the recitation of the charm. A charm functioning as a remedy for worms, found in *The Long Hidden Friend*, illustrates this well:

---

53 I strongly advise a person wishing to pick up the practice of narrative charms to seek them out in their own native tradition and in their own native tongue. It is highly recommended that you find a living teacher who embodies the tradition and can empower you with the charms directly; however, just setting out and using them yourself, with genuine respect and care in a needed situation should be enough to get you in touch with their underlying power, which is made available by re-connecting to the tradition. In other words, none of the English translations given in this book should be of any practical use to you, and are only included as examples of structure and content.

Mary, God's Mother, traversed the land,
Holding three worms close in her hand;
One was white, the other was black, the third was red
This must be repeated three times, at the same time
stroking the person or animal with the hand; and at the
end of each application strike the back of the person or the
animal, to wit: at the first application once, at the second
application twice, and at the third application three times;
and then set the worms a certain time, but not less than
three minutes.[54]

The verbal, visual and physical actions overlap and become
one single experience. The scenario of the narrative can perhaps
be understood as a 'world' in and of itself, which plays out its reality
in a given situation. It bleeds through and permeates the moment,
uniting the actions at work in the narrative with those undertaken
in the material world. This multi-dimensional cognitive approach
is usually a given within magical praxis, yet it is also one of its
most misunderstood features. For example, we see similar additions
of incantations recited and inscribed along with a corresponding
ritual practice among the ancient Greco-Roman method involving
so-called *defixiones*. These are typically lead tablets ritually engraved
with what could be defined as performative statements, which were
ritually repeated at the time of their creation and consecration.
For instance, on a Roman tablet of this type we find the following
words inscribed:

---

54 John George Hohman *The Long Hidden Friend* (Troy Books, 2013), p.
31.

Malchio, son of Nico: his eyes, hands, fingers... I pierce[55]

This curse would probably have been sealed with the actual piercing of the lead tablet and/or a poppet connecting it to the victim. We find similar examples of binding, drowning, and disposing in various dreary places such as tombs and so on, where the textual inscription is linked to the action undertaken and the wished-for result. This exemplifies how verbal, textual, and physical actions are conjoined with other similar practices, producing a unified, multimedial, and multi-dimensional vehicle for the work to play out. By integrating all these various expressions of power and intent together, the ritual aim is amplified and diversified and one thus seeks to cover as many levels of projection as possible in one unified process. Most significantly, the spiritual and mental properties at work are managed via the use of all these media at the same time as the physical process is completed. The sorcerer thus operates on several levels of reality at once by means of various forms of tools and techniques, weaving them all into one whole. They all express and give physical shape to a happening which essentially takes place *within* his or her consciousness, extending it outwards and solidifying the process on another plane of action.

---

55 DTAud 135 = AE 1989: 319, quoted in Amina Kropp, *How Does Magical Language Work?*, p. 361.

A narrative charm which perfectly exemplifies this multi-dimensional approach can be found in the Tibetan *Kangyur* or canonical collection of translated sayings of the Buddha, which combines *Varjayana* ritual methodology and technology with pre-tantric Buddhist magic.[56] As should be noted, it weaves together the narrative with mantric recitation, functioning as a single sonic formula to be performed together with a physical ritual action:

Homage to all the Buddhas and Bodhisattvas!
I heard this one time, when the Transcendent Conqueror
[i.e. the Buddha] was seated along with a great assembly
of about five hundred gelong or fully ordained monks in
the sacred Bamboo Grove in Kalandaka in Rajagrha.
Right when the moon was full on the fifteenth day of
the lunar calendar, the day of monastic sojong or vow
confession/reparation rites, the Transcendent Conqueror
sat on a seat laid out in front of the sangha. At that time,
the Venerable disciple [literally 'the one endowed with
life'] Ananda held an animal tail fly-whisk about the
Buddha's person. He waved it in his direction and sat
down. Then the Venerable Ananda draped his monastic
shawl or upper garment over one shoulder and pressed
his right kneecap into the ground. He turned towards
where the Buddha was and bowing and pressing his
palms together entreated the Buddha as follows:
'Transcendent Conqueror! Here in Rajagrha there
are many monks who have piles, who are pained
by the disease of hemorrhoids. When these monks

---

56 The use of the *historiolae* within early Buddhist magic was most probably drawn from pre-Buddhistic material such as that found within the Atharaveda, as explored in the previous chapter. (See *Buddhist Magic*, chapter 1, by Sam Van Schaik.)

experience intense and unbearable suffering, when they experience discomfort and repellent feelings, Disciplined Transcendent Conqueror, what can I do for them?'
Thus he implored him.
The Transcendent Conqueror bestowed the following advice on Venerable Ananda:
'O you Venerable Ananda, take up this sutra for eliminating haemorrhoids. Whosoever knows the name, words, and letters of this sutra for eliminating haemorrhoids shall never be affected by the disease of piles for as long as they shall live. It shall be remembered for up to seven life-times:
TADYATA ALANTÉ ALAMÉ SVALICINI KUSHI SAMBHAVA SVAHA

'Look here, Ananda. To the North, on the King of Mountains called 'Snow[y]', there is a Sala tree known as 'Completely Victorious', which has three flowers. The first is called 'Proliferating'. The second is called 'Soft' or 'Gentle'. The third is called 'Dry'.
In just this way, let the swellings of all sentient beings connected with the loong or wind humour be dried up in kind! Let their tripa or bile-related swellings be dried up! Let their bedken or phlegm-related swellings dry up! Let their impure swellings dry up! Let their blood-filled swellings dry up! Let their combined humour swellings dry up! Let their nasal swellings dry up! Let their dangling or prolapsed swellings be dried up!
TADYATA SHAMÉ SHAMĀNÉ SHAMÉ SHAMĀNÉ SVAHA

May there be no pain or sickness! May there be no
numbness or paralysis! May no sounds come forth! May
there be no leakage! May there be no pain! May there be
no exceeding suffering! May there be no contamination
or deterioration! May there be no utter contamination
or deterioration! May just this [affliction] deteriorate and
completely exhaust itself! May it cease to exist! May it
disappear beneath the earth!
NAMO BHAGAVATÉ BUDDHAYA SATYAVATINAM
SIDDHYANTU MANTRAPADANI SVAHA'
After the Buddha bestowed this advice, Ananda
rejoiced. He fully and directly praised the words of the
Transcendent Conqueror.
And so, this is the ritual:
Having completely read this sutra, recite it seven times
over a red thread. [Tying] seven knots, fasten it around
your neck.[57]

In practice there is not much of a difference between the
historiolae and any other types of incantation or *voces magica*. They
can all be perceived as expressions or embodiments of occult power,
and can be applied with more or less precision dependent on the
magician's ability to function as a catalyst and mediator of such
power. What makes them special is their emphasis on motion and
a specified movement of this power. When calling on the aid of a
divine power by uttering a specific divine name, their wanted actions
must most often be specified additionally. The *historiola*, however,
in and of itself functioning as an incantation, is pre-arranged in
terms of what specific actions the being should perform and to what

---

57 Unpublished translation by Ben Joffe, shared privately with the author,
25 August, 2020.

outcome. The narrative is already given, and sets the stage for how the magical operation is to be played out. Like a channel that allows a stream to run through it, the *historiola* presents a structure through which the energies at hand can flow. As with the Tibetan charm given above, the mantras provided are given further empowerment through the narrative as it moves the mantric utterance into a clear and precise setting, which includes further points of entry and specifications to amplify the magical process.

We should not come to think of these charms as in any way rigid or mechanical; just because they have a defined structure does not mean they are not dynamic in nature or cannot be used for a multiplicity of ends. Not only did we see how adaptable to cultural and religious contexts these charms are in the last chapter, but also how fluid they are in terms of use. An identical over-arching narrative can be utilized to cure both the evil eye as well as migraine, showing how performers of these practices have been open to adapting the charms to a large variety of afflictions and situations. A charm which is theoretically set out to cure the well-being of farmyard cattle could in practice also be applied to heal a human being and vice versa.[58] Similarly, charms which explicitly state that they are for the healing of physical injuries can be used practically to soothe psychological issues or to drive off demonic influences from a client. In the Trolldom tradition, practitioners would not normally use more than one or two troll formulas on a regular basis; any more than that would simply be thought superfluous. Of course, taking into account how well-protected these charms were and how difficult it must have been to obtain them in a widely illiterate rural society without any textual sources at hand, it is not strange that one had to make do with the few methods one had available. A small number of charms is still to this day (where access

---

58 See for example *Svartkonstböcker* by Dr. Thomas K. Johnsson, p. 321-22.

to textual sources is abundant) seen as absolutely sufficient, as they, without any kind of formulaic alteration whatsoever, are used for a wide multiplicity of needs. It is simply the imagination, intention, and ability of the practitioner which set the limits of their use.

WORDS AS WORLDS

If I am correct in asserting that it is somewhat deceptive to regard the dimension of temporality as a fundamentally significant trait of the *historiolae*, then what are we to do with the significance of spatiality? I would propose that this is a worthwhile aspect to look into more deeply, as it at least to some degree says something more accurate about their phenomenological structure. With that in mind, I would like to begin this chapter by quoting a beautiful narrative charm from the Russian folk magical tradition, traditionally used to heal wounds:

> I will rise, servant of God (name), blessing myself, I
> will go, crossing myself, from the hut by way of the
> doors, from the yard by way of the gates, into the open
> field beyond the gates. In the open field there stands a
> holy ocean-stone, on that holy ocean-stone there sits a
> red maiden with a silken thread, she sews the wound,
> removes the sting, and charms the blood of God's
> servant (name), and so that there be no more stinging,
> nor breaking, nor swelling, by my word, lock and key,
> from now to forever.[59]

---

59 Joseph L. Conrad, 'Russian Ritual Incantations', *The Slavic and East European Journal*, 33.3 (Autumn, 1989), 429.

Let us examine the highly evocative use of locality and movement within this charm. First and foremost, the practitioner is to rise up, spiritually awake as on a new day, breaking off from the previous moment and its mundane features with a sense of clarity and focus, to perform a specific action. Stating her name and pronouncing herself as a servant of God, armed and protected under His blessing, she now ventures out beyond her farm and proceeds into an 'open field'. This field is essentially what could be understood as the 'stage' for the narrative to take place. It is not only a meeting point for the 'worldly' and the 'otherworldly', but even moreso a space which is reserved for magical operation and where one can encounter and access entities of profound power. Next, the practitioner finds an ocean-stone, a 'burning' stone which perhaps is none other than what Russian folklore calls the *Alatyr* and which according to yet another narrative charm can be found on the mystical island known as *Bujan*.[60] The focus, from the action and movement of the practitioner, has at this point switched to those of the maiden and her healing powers. It is this maiden, not the practitioner, who takes care of healing a client, yet nowhere is it stated that the client is present until this very moment. I propose that this is because this is where the actual overlapping of the two realms happens; they conjoin, as it were, and are brought together in a single action. The practitioner verbally (and subsequently mentally) travels to a place where she meets a being who holds a

---

60 The reason for me proposing this is because both charms describe how a red maiden sits upon such a stone: 'On the ocean, on the sea, on the island of Bujan there lies a white burning stone Alatyr', on that stone, Alatyr', there sits a red maiden, a master seamstress, she holds a steel needle, threads it with a silken thread, into the dark-yellow blood, she sews the bloody wounds. I do charm the cut away from the servant (name). Steel stand back, and you, blood, cease to flow.' Conrad, 'Russian Ritual Incantations', 429.

power strong enough heal the wound. This power is now made readily available to the practitioner, who is then able to bring it forth into the physical realm by continuing to recite the charm and also optionally performing other healing actions such as the actual cleaning and stitching of the physical wound.

Again, all of this simply happens by means of uttering words. There is no so-called astral travel taking place, no spirits summoned in triangles, nor any elaborate prayers spoken (even though this is paradoxically mentioned in the charm itself). The narrative allows all of these happenings to take place in an extremely condensed and accessible manner. What we have to understand is that the charm functions as a carrier and vessel for these actions, yet they are expressed almost as a distilled and explicated retelling of such events. For this to happen, the practitioner needs to be firm in intention, but perhaps more importantly, in imagination, and must have a great deal of sensibility in terms of how unseen forces can be moved and directed via the spoken word. In relation to our Russian charm, the practitioner has to fully experience and *perceive* the workings of the red maiden. This is made possible by the journey the practitioner has made to a place where such perception can be vividly established: in this case atop the holy stone, in the open field, beyond her farm. This perception is the direct sensation of the power at work, and it is this which the charmer manages to convey with the charm, passing it via their mind and words into the physical world. That which previously was distant and 'otherworldly' has now become present and tangible, accessible for the sorcerer to implement as he or she pleases. This is why it is important to note that the agents and forces mentioned in the charms are not simply hypothetical, nor are they 'analogies': they are direct influences which are encountered and made perceivable, via the expression as verbal concepts. As narratives, they are worlds which open up within the consciousness of the practitioner, concretized as words.

It might come as a surprise, then, that the perception spoken of here is not specifically a visual one. It can of course entail such a dimension, but ultimately I am mainly referring to a specific force, which the entity in the narrative wields whilst performing its action. Still, as we have seen, this action is given a surrounding, a locality, and a context when presented in a narrative form. This helps guide the imagination of the practitioner, and gives that which is highly subtle and almost abstract a form that can be more easily encountered and connected with. It also presents the benefit of a certain cognitive apprehension of organizing, structuring, and navigating principles in a 'space'. Our minds naturally and spontaneously organize the abstract and the formless into spatio-temporal principles, producing both vague and clear conceptual images and words. The charms essentially present a structured screen upon which the mind can grasp the normally ungraspable, formulating a pathway through which energy can flow. The spatial aspect of the *historiola* thus functions as a means of projection of the super-spatial dimensions of reality onto the world of everyday life. This aspect is not only needed for us to integrate the lofty powers which are sought out in the charms within a graspable perception of external reality, but is also ingeniously used to accomplish highly specified aims. For instance, in the charms involving a meeting between a holy figure and demonic entity, they always meet at a road. The ill-natured being has, in other words, not yet reached its final destination and is still in a state of transition. Its wicked intent has thus not come to full fruition and can be warded off and sent back on the same road as it came. This, of course, would be a natural preference if the aim is to counter a curse sent off by an enemy or the like, or to return the influences of the evil eye. It can also (which is more commonly found among the charms) be sent off to another destination completely. This type of charm would be used when dealing with a natural illness which is *not* sent out directly by any human agent. In the Norse charms these are usually locations such as 'The Blue Mountain' (see chapter one), the furthest north, a lake on which no one rows, on a mountain upon which no one lives, under a great stone where nothing grows, and so on.[61] These are obviously places which should be thought of as meaning something like 'as far away as possible, and where you can no longer hurt anyone'. However, when formulated, it also gives the practitioner a somewhat concrete sense of what such a place is like, which should hopefully give the command more substance and force. A Slovenian charm against bone tuberculosis reads:

> Go to a maple tree, From the maple to a leaf, From the leaf to a mountain, Where no bell tolls, No chair stands, No butt sits, No fire cooks, No mouth eats. There you stay, this is not where you belong! I beseech you in the name of the Father, the Son and the Holy Ghost.[62]

The illness and the pain, as an entities or substances, are thus commanded to go elsewhere, to take flight and seek another physical (or at least 'imaginal') place to reside. It should move from one place to another, as in a chain, making it more and more difficult to return to the bone where it is currently causing problems.

----

61 Note how the ancient charm against migraine mentioned by Barb (quoted in chapter 2) uses a similar structure. First the demonic entity is commanded to take flight unto a wild mountain, and instead of going after a human host, Jesus demands that it should use the head of a bull as a 'substitute'. Yet if the demon does not continue to obey this command and tries to escape the substitute host, Jesus states that he will utterly destroy it instead. In other words, we begin with a negotiation, but if this does not work, we move on to threat. By stating all this 'at once' in the charm, the practitioner has thus secured all loose ends of the exorcism.

62 Monika Kropej, 'Charms in the context of magic practice. The case of Slovenia', *Folklore* 24 (2003), 64.

Many times, this sort of command also entails a temporal dimension, as in demanding the entity remains in such a place 'as long as the world stands' or until Judgement Day. The following charm from Latvia, used to bind a thief, very well exemplifies this temporal aspect:

Our Mother of God walked over a green field and the child of God was by her hand. Then came three thieves who wanted to steal that baby. And she started to scream: 'bind, Peter, bind!' Peter replied: 'I've bound them not with chains but holy hands of God. You shall stand like a log and here you shall count all stars in heaven, all leaves on trees, all stones on the field and all sand on the seashore. You shall stand and move no further until I come and release you. In the name of...[63]

This brings yet another binding element to the charm, as it sets out the parameters of time to make sure that all aspects of the procedure are covered and clarified. This 'internal' spatial and temporal dimension to the charms enables the transference into the 'outer' realm, binding them into one world instead of two separate realities. Instead of being abstractions, the scenarios can be traced and imagined as taking place in the physical world, although many times being loaded with a highly miraculous content.

Some of the charms that we have previously explored do not include any elaborate movement between worlds or 'introductions' at all. In these, the characters just seem to appear out of thin air, wandering out of nowhere to perform their actions without any real contextual backdrop, like a character acting out a *deus ex machina* in

---

63 Toms Ķencis, 'Angels, Thieves and Narratives: A case study of Latvian thief binding charms', *Incantatio* 8 (2019), 7.

a play. The following charm recorded in London by Samuel Pepys in 1664 illustrates this well:

There came Three Angels out of the East; The one brought fire, the other brought frost – Out fire; in frost, In the name of Father, and Son, and Holy Ghost. Amen.[64]

The powers at work within these charms are immediately instantiated and 'projected' upon the physical realm, without any prolonged imaginative support; however, in practice there are no real differences between these and the more elaborate examples. Although 'lacking' in a complex style and broad structure, they focus on the bare essentials of what the charmer aims to accomplish. More condensed charms can thus be considered to be preferred in terms of their utility (they simply take less time to utter), yet could on the other hand be thought to leave too much to chance. Ultimately though, this is mainly a matter of personal taste and skill, and there is nothing to say that similar magical components found in the longer charms could not be performed by the practitioner along with the shorter charms. It is interesting to note that even in some of the most condensed *historiolae*, the characters are said to 'come walking', or are 'arriving', as if they still need to be introduced into a given scenario. The description of their movement upon the scene functions in a way as an evocation of sorts, bringing them into the domain of the given situation. This also establishes the characters as 'outside' influences, and their unknown origin conveys a certain air of being armed with mysterious skills and powers.

---

64 Venetia Newall, *Encyclopedia of Witchcraft and Magic* (London: Hamlyn, 1974), p. 51.

We could think of these more extensive charms as explicitly stating the methodology of the magical process, whilst the shorter either lack it or hold it as implicit. If we affirm the notion that words are actions, that language can have a performative function, and that words can also be carriers of metaphysical power, we can see how the structure of the narratives are essentially verbalized rituals in and of themselves. From this perspective, many preconceptions regarding the nature of magic must be reconsidered, as we are met with a deeply ingenious form of esoteric practice where vocal utterance or the written word can even substitute for physical action. The internal world of the mind has the ability to directly connect us with those miraculous powers which are typically unnoticeable to the common exteriorized senses, and can in this manner bridge the world of spirit and the world of matter. The imaginative force set in motion by the charm is thus perceived as utterly real in an ontological sense, and its transference manifests as something highly substantial to the practitioner, albeit in a subtle and occult sense. The word, and the process conducted by means of its recitation, is evoked in the consciousness of the magician, and as such it holds a potential to also be transferred onto the reality of, for instance, the body of a patient. The practitioner has access to certain metaphysical worlds, like true dreams, which when relived (recited) act out a certain natural truth as a dynamic energetic process.

For instance, the process which is implicitly sought out when speaking the concluding words 'lock and key' in the Russian charm above, formulates the performance of sealing and finalizing the magical action as a whole. It draws the mind into the precise cognitive 'motion' or sensation which is linked to the performance of turning a key in a lock, and uses this as a means of establishing a certain reality. It is in this sense a dynamic form which flows into the realm of other forms, and as it is conceived of as similarly real, it has the ability to change the course of happenings on that plane. As noted earlier, behind this notion lies an understanding of the ontological possibilities of imagination and how principles alive within one's consciousness can move and basically be 'placed' at will within space. Yet it is not the world of the charm which is sought out essentially, but rather the happenings or powers at work within it. The world, or the frame-story, gives the practitioner a point of imaginative access to these powers, in a clear and comprehensive manner. It conveys a structure of reality, or a model through which certain energies come alive, and allows the magician to draw on these in the here and now. Scholar Edina Bozóky summarizes this in the following comparison:

> In non-narrative charms, the desired state, cure or protection is expressed by a conjuration, a direct order addressed to supernatural evil powers or to the sickness. The officiating person, the healer, assumes here the role of mediator between the sick man or woman and the malevolent forces. In narrative charms, a story—even very nuclear—introduces the conjuring formula. Here, the supernatural healing power is transferred, at least in part, to the protagonist of the micro-story.[65]

The worlds and the images of the various charms might, however, not be 'supernatural' or 'mythic'. As we have seen, one may equally draw on aspects of the world of animals (as in the charm of the wolf quoted in chapter two), of natural phenomena ('as dew before the sun'), or the everyday world of human affairs ('lock and key'). Essentially, anything that can stimulate a certain preferred mental motion can be utilized. Often this is a matter of a

---

65 Bozóky, 'Medieval Narrative Charms', 112.

complex internal logic, which can vary significantly due to cultural contexts and individual leanings. For example here is a Roman healing charm, which makes use of a rather peculiar imagery:

A mule cannot propagate, a stone cannot make wool[66]

This is followed by a command to also reduce the illness to a state of non-existence, as these empirical facts also emphasize. But as the charms function as structures of reality, their internal logic is but a means to reveal the performative essence. The Roman charm can in one sense be seen as altogether absurd, but when considering that what the practitioner seeks is a state of affairs where a certain aspect of reality is made illogical and non-existent, it actually makes it highly *logical*. Now, it might be easy for us to think of this as a formulation of an analogy, which states 'as X, so Y'; however, I would argue that we should instead think of this as a matter of an evocation of a certain power, or a certain aspect of reality. In this case, a principle of 'non-existence' or natural incomprehension is to be made manifest via the negative assertions regarding the mule and the stone.[67] The illness is to be both mentally and physically positioned in the same negative domain as these things, thus being made powerless by its complete lack of substance and existence.

Sometimes, however, the natural world around us might not seem 'enough'. The problem arising might be something which seems to be out of our ordinary reach, and outside of our ordinary points of reference. Perhaps the issue might even be considered to be of a nature distinct from the domain of normal human life

---

66 Versnel, 'The Poetics of the Magical Charm', p. 128.

67 Ironically, there have been odd, documented cases in modern times of mules propagating, but this perhaps demonstrates how much of the logic of the charms is indeed linked to a specific cultural context and an internal logic.

altogether. In this case, we will need to bring forth a suitable type of power, matching the given situation. The world of myth is an arena of reference that encapsulates living spiritual agency, and when properly understood from a magical perspective, brings the commonly inconceivable to life and opens up new vistas of possibility. Here, the power does not come from the limited scope of our egos, but from a well-spring of otherworldly energy and unfailing potency. When evoking such a realm into our mental landscape, we are in direct contact with the mechanics of healing which knows no limits and is steadfast regardless of our own frail human nature. When the narrative is spoken, it reveals a possibility to access this potency, which would otherwise be closed to us. The 'imaginary' presents us with a truth more potent than the conventionally conceived limits of the material world. As when we read a book of fiction, a work of poetry, or see a film which grants us new metaphors to examine and understand our own experience of reality, myths reveal the world as a wider realm of supra-mundane interaction. They provide us with tools to comprehend and refer to the occulted dimension of life by formulating the unseen as something tangible and approachable. The practice of the *historiolae*, however, informs us that this can not only be experienced in a sentimental and metaphorical manner, but also in a highly direct sense. If our imagination can bring us closer to something that is genuinely real on an emotional or theoretical level, why should it not also be able to connect us with a layer of reality which can have effects on the physical world?

❦

As magic is an art that directly makes use of our dynamic imagination, the notion of a 'story' can become a profound tool for the magician. When understanding that our ordinary conception of the world is in one sense merely a giant story, told via words, thoughts, and sense organs, we likewise arrive at the realization that we can re-arrange the settings of the stage upon which it is retold. We can alter the script of life with the lines of greater playwrights, drawing on their expressions of reality in order to merge them with our own experience. As humans, we need structures, words, and images to fathom and come to terms with the chaos of the world we inhabit. We need to formulate them in ways that make sense and have meaning to us – inspiring and moving us in a manner that is useful to our everyday needs. We share a bond, or at least a form of closeness with these models of reality, otherwise they have played out their roles. To understand a myth is perhaps first and foremost about understanding our relationship with the characters, and what arises in us as we tell or listen to the narrative. What emotions are stirred? What ideas come to life? What new perspectives are presented to us? The charms discussed in this book can be thought to function in a similar manner, yet they naturally force this notion to its most radical conclusion – namely, that the mythic stories are as real as the stories of our daily lives. As magic is the art of articulating, accessing, and utilizing occult power, the *historiola* must be viewed as a supreme example of this craft, as it both expresses as well as performs the magical action at the same time. Like the three maidens who spin and unravel the cords of destiny, the art of magic enables us to conceive of our lives not only through the concepts and stories that others have given us by the mundane structures of society, but we are also set free to fashion a world from the outlook of perpetual wonder. Note though that this is not a world of relativism, fairy-tale, and make-believe, but paradoxically a world free from grasping after the fictions that we commonly perceive as fundamental to how the universe works. True myths can lead us into a space – into a world – where we can discover previously inconceivable potential and power. All we need to do is remain open to the possibilities which come alive *through* our imagination, but are ultimately not *of it*. By allowing this space into our lives we become more attentive to the raw, natural energy that blazes forth like sparks from the movement and actions of the great forces of nature and spirit alike. Over time, this gives way to a deeper, natural comprehension of the closeness of the relationship between our awareness and these dynamic forces, and we see how hard it is to exclude their presence from our everyday lives. This is when all of our daily actions start to merge with the flow of wonder and true magic – our lives transformed in constant myths – and where we become partakers and heroes in the grand story which is the Universe Itself.

BIBLIOGRAPHY

Arill, David (ed), *Bohuslänska Folkminnen: Studier och Upptäckningar* (Uddevalla, 1922)

Bang, Anton Christian, *Norske Hexeformularer og Magiske Opskrifter* (Norway: Kristiana, 1902)

Barb, A.A., *Antaura. The Mermaid and the Devil's Grandmother: A Lecture* in *Journal of the Warburg and Courtauld Institutes,* Vol. 29 (1966)

Betz, Hans Dieter, *The Greek Magical Papyri in Translation: Including the Demotic Spells: Volume 1 Texts* (Chicago: University of Chicago Press, 1996)

Bohak, Gideon, 'The Uses of Cosmogonic Myths in Ancient Jewish Magic', in *Archiv für Religionsgeschichte*, Vol. 13 (De Gruyter 2012)

Bozóky, Edina, 'Medieval Narrative Charms Medieval Narrative Charms', in James A. Kapalo, Eva Pocs and William F. Ryan (eds), *The Power of Words: Studies on Charms and Charming in Europe* (Budapest: Central European University, 2013)

Conrad, Joseph L., 'Russian Ritual Incantations: Tradition, Diversity and Continuity', *The Slavic and East European Journal*, 33.3 (1989)

Davies, Owen, 'Healing Charms in Use in England and Wales 1700-1950', in *Folklore* Vol. 107 (Taylor & Francis, Ltd. 1996)

Davies, Owen, *Grimoires: A History of Magic Books* (Oxford: Oxford University Press 2009)

Ek, Sverker, *Bohuslänska Vallvisor in Bohuslänska Folkminnen: Studier och Upptäckningar* (Uddevalla: Hallmans Boktryckeri A., 1922)

Eliade, Mircea, *Myth and Reality*, trans. by Willard A. Trask (New York: Colophon-Harper & Row, 1963)

Frankfurter, David, *'Narrating Power: The theory and practice of the magical historiola in ritual spells'*, in P. Mirecki & M. Meyer (eds), *Ancient Magic and Ritual Power* (Brill 1995)

Frazer, Sir James George, *The Golden Bough: The Magic Art* Vol. 1 (New York: MacMillan & Co., 1951)

Gårdbäck, Johannes Björn, *Trolldom: Spells and methods of the Norse folk magic tradition* (YIPPIE, 2015)

Graf, Fritz, 'Historiola', in *Brill's New Pauly* (Brill Online, 2006)

Grendon, Felix, 'Anglo-Saxon Charms', in *Journal of American Folklore* 22.84 (University of Toronto, 1909)

Griffith, Ralph T.H., *Hymns of the Atharva-Veda* (London: E. J. Lazarus and Co. 1895)

Hohman, John George, *The Long Hidden Friend* (London: Troy Books, 2013)

Iamblichus, *On the Mysteries*, trans. by Emma C. Clarke, John M. Dillon, and Jackson P. Hershbell (Society of Biblical Literature, 2003)

Johnson, Thomas K., S*vartkonstböcker: A Compendium of the Swedish Black Art Book Tradition* (Seattle: Revelore Press, 2019)

L. Kákosy, 'Remarks on the Interpretation of a Coptic Magical Text', *Acta Orientalia*, 13 (1961)

Ķencis, Toms, 'Angels, Thieves and Narratives: A case study of Latvian thief binding charms', *Incantatio*, 8 (2019)

King, Graham, *The British Book of Spells and Charms* (London: Troy Books, 2016)

Kropej, Monika, 'Charms in the context of magic practice. The case of Slovenia', *Folklore* 24 (2003), 64.

Kropp, Amina, 'How does magical language work? The spells and formulae of the Latin defixionum tabellae', in F.M. Simón & R. Gordon (eds), *Magical Practice in the Latin West* (Brill, 2009)

Lindow, John, *Norse Mythology: A Guide to Gods, Heroes, Rituals, and Beliefs* (Oxford: Oxford University Press, 2001)

Newall, Venetia, *Encyclopedia of Witchcraft and Magic* (London: Hamlyn, 1974)

Macbain, Alexander, 'Gaelic Incantation', in *Transactions of the Gaelic Society of Inverness* (1892)

Mercer, A.D., *The Wicked Shall Decay: Charms, Spell & Witchcraft of Old Britain* (California: Three Hands Press, 2018)

Ohrt, Ferdinand, *Danmarks Trylleformler* Vol 1-2 (Gyldendal, 1917)

Ritner, Robert K., *The Mechanics of Ancient Egyptian Magical Practice*, Series: Studies in Ancient Oriental Civilizations, 54 (Chicago: Oriental Institute, 1993)

Sanders, Seth L., 'A Historiography of Demons: Preterit-Thema, Para-Myth, and Historiola in Morphology Genres', in Tzvi Abusch (ed), *Proceedings of the XLV Rencontre Assyriologique Internationale: Historiography in the Cuneiform World* (Bethesda, Md.: CDL Press, 2001)

Staal, Frits, *Discovering the Vedas: Origins, Mantras, Rituals, Insights* (New York: Penguin, 2009)

Véronèse, Julien, 'Magic, Theurgy, and Spirituality in the Medieval Ritual of the Ars notoria', in Claire Fanger (ed), *Invoking Angels: Theurgic Ideas and Practices, Thirteenth to Sixteenth Centuries* (Pennsylvania: Penn State University Press, 2012)

Versnel, H.S., 'The poetics of the magical charm – an essay in the words of power', in P. Mirecki & M. Meyer (ed), *Magic in the Ancient World* (Leiden: Brill 2001)

Van Schaik, Sam, *Buddhist Magic: Divination, Healing, and Enchantment through the Ages* (Boulder: Shambhala, 2020)

INDEX